Vincent Lamantia

Latest Official Map and Guide of Guatemala and Honduras

A short history of the thrifty republic of the south

Vincent Lamantia

Latest Official Map and Guide of Guatemala and Honduras
A short history of the thrifty republic of the south

ISBN/EAN: 9783337314200

Printed in Europe, USA, Canada, Australia, Japan

Cover: Foto ©ninafisch / pixelio.de

More available books at **www.hansebooks.com**

LATEST OFFICIAL
MAP AND GUIDE
~∞ OF ∞~
Guatemala and Honduras

Jose Maria Reina Barrios,
President of Guatemala.

A Short History of the thrifty Republic of the South, containing all information that will be useful to the visitor, immigrant and workingman.

...ISSUED BY...
V. LAMANTIA LABOR AGENT,
327 Exchange Alley,   New Orleans, La.

To his Excellency,

JOSE MARIA REINA BARRIOS,

President of Guatemala.

This little *work* is respectfully
dedicated as a slight acknowledge-
ment of the many sterling qualities
of the most **progressive** ruler of
that Republic.

VINCENT LAMANTIA.

Ex. U. S. Consul,

Catania, Scicily.

GUATEMALA.

A SHORT HISTORY OF THE THRIFTY REPUBLIC OF THE SOUTH.

Containing All Information that Will Be Useful to the Visitor, Immigrant and Working Man.

If there is a country where progress and prosperity walk hand in hand, and over which the shadow of coming events now rests, Guatemala is that country. It is the El Dorado of the laboring man and a mine of wealh to the visitor. No lack of work, no want of money.

`A history of the origin of Guatemala will, of course, will be of no interest or moment to those who labor long for a livelihood. The following

brief sketch of the state is therefore
appended for the benefit of those who
may wish to visit that country of
sights and signs as a matter of education or amusement.

In 1502 Columbus, the great navigator, landed on the coast of what is
now known as Honduras, and took
possession of that country in the name
of Spain. In 1523 Cortez, after con-
quoring Mexico, sent one of his offi-
cers south. This officer made himself
master of the northern portion of
Central America, or what is now
known as the state of Guatemala.
This was virtually the origin and beginning of the country now attracting
so much attention. In the course of
a few years all the country south, em-
bracing the present five Central American states, was under the control of
Spain, and was organized under the
captain generalship of Guatemala, the
other states being provinces.

In 1820-21 Guatemala, or Central
America, shook off the Spanish yoke,
and for a time was a part of Mexico.
In 1824 the Republic of Central America was formed by a union of all the
states, but this was dissolved in 1839
by the withdrawal of Honduras and
Nicaragua. Matters continued in this
state until 1872, when President Bar-
nos (uncle of the present ruler), the
President of Guatemala, made an ef-
fort to form a federation of all the

states, under the general name of the
United States of Central America.
Jealousy of the other states and sus-
picion of the President's motive
caused dissention in the other states,
and eventually led to war, in which
Barrios, the originator of the great
movement, lost his life, being killed
in the battle of Chalchuapa, in 1885.

War and bloodshed continued in
this portion of the world for some
years, and this continued strife has
tended to retard the development of
the country. It has remained for Jose
Maria Reina Barrios, the present
ruler, to carry into effect a movement
for the settlement and civilization.

Guatemala is the most important of
the five Central American Republics.
It is third in size, but first in agricultural and commercial importance. It
has an estimated area of 46,800 square
miles. There are twenty-seven depart-
mnts or counties, and there are 374
cities and towns, and in 1870 had a
population of 1,394,223. ´

By the amended constitution of 1889
executive power is vested in a President, who is elected for six years, and
a National Assembly, elected for four
years. These are all chosen by universal suffrage, the same as in the
United States.

The physical aspect of Guatemala is
generally mountainous. The mouns-
tains are covered with magnificent

forests, and from this the state takes its name, as the meaning of "Guatemala" is "full of trees."

The country has a great variety of climates. On the Pacific coast the heat is intense. On the Atlantic side it is much cooler. As one leaves the seashore the climate changes and becomes cooler as the distance increases. It is cold in the highlands, and sometimes snows. The maximum temperature is 88 degrees, the minimum 38 degrees, the average 65 degrees.

VARIOUS ALTITUDES.

The city of Guatemala has an altitude of about 6,000 feet, same as the City of Mexico.

Amatitlan has an altitude of 4,212 feet. Escuintla has has about the same. It is a popular health and summer resort of the state.

Antigua is one of the historic cities of the state. It was fonded in 1583. It is surrounded by rich lands, and is the center of the vast sugar and coffee interests. It has an elevation of 5,000 feet.

Chimaltenango is also a large and wealthy city. Here are located vast cotton factories, and other industries. It has an elevation of about 3,000 feet.

The city of Coban has an elevation of 4,300 feet. It is the center of vast coffee and fruit interests.

Zacapa is located in a fertile valley. It is a city of 44,000 people. It has an elevation of 600 feet. It is healthy and the climate agreeable.

Chiquimula is about the same elevation as Zacapa. It has a population of 63,000.

Jalapa has an elevation of 6,000 feet. The climate is even, being very little change the year around. Agriculture is the prinncipal industry.

Jutiapa is low, but the climate is healthy, although warm. Coffee and sugar is the principal industry.

The towns mentioned are along the line of the railroad, and a very clear idea can thus be had of the climate, etc., along the line.

IMMIGRATION.

Guatemala is a healthy country, abundant in vacant and fertile lands, almost two-thirds of which are not cultivated for want of labor, and the country offers to immigrants great advantages. The soil needs no fertilizers, and the industrious immigrant even without capital, will simply have to till the land slightly and sow the grani to obtain a sufficient crop after six months for the ample support of a family.

The government encourages and protects immigration in a very liberal manner. Those who possess a little money can make a fortune within a few years. Others who have a profession or trade find unlimited fields to exercise them profitably. No person ever yet left the country on account of a want of an opportunity to invest his capital or for lack of lucrative employment, when he wanted to work.

A few years ago a vessel with Italian immigrants arrived in Guatemala and though nothing was prepared for them, every one found employment without difficulty. Those who had no money, made a good living cutting grass from the fields and selling it in the cities. Others cultivated gardens, and did well with vegetables, etc. Others raised pigs, chickens, etc., and made money.

THE PURCHASE OF LANDS.

The following are the principal articles of the code concerning the purchase of vacant lands:

Two dollars per hectare ($2\frac{1}{2}$ acres), if the lands are level and covered with natural pasture.

One dollar and a half if the land is level and covered with brush, from which sassaparilla, gutta-percha, etc., can be obtained.

One dollar if there are no bushes, but none of the above products.

Eighty cents if the lands are broken, stony, etc.

Lands that are within sixty miles of a city are appraised at about one-quarter increase.

The appraisement of lands is made by experts.

COST OF ARTICLES OF FAMILY USE.

Fresh beef, 8 cents; coffee, 12 cents; flour, $8 per hundred pounds; butter, 40 cents per pound; tobacco, 40 cents per pound; soap, 10 cents; oranges, per 100, 15 cents; eggs, 10 cents; wood for fuel, 30 cents per load.

Animals.

Horses, $40 to $80; mules, $60 to $320; cattle, average price, $14.

Wages are never less than $1 per day.

All the prices here gaven are in Guatemala money.

HOW TO GO.

In former days the trip from the United States to Guatemala was a matter of serious thought, and consumed much time. Steamers only left New York at irregular, intervals, and the time was something over fourteen days, and the fare was $45. Passengers were compelled to go by the Isthmus of Panama and up thePacific side to San Jose. Now the trip is a small matter of five days, with comfort and ease, and the cost is $30 or $18. For this shortening of time the public is indebted to the New Orleans, Belize and Royal Mail Steamship Company of New Orleans, and known as the Machica line. The fleet is composed of five steamers, and was organized by Messrs John and Mike Macheca known as the "Macheca Bros." At the beginning there were only two vessels.

The present personnel of the line is John and Mike Macheca, Joe and Peter Torre, Mr D. Cifalu, John B. Cifalu and Captain Leech. All enterprising people, to whom Guatemala owes much of her progress and prosperity.

The vessels now composing the Machica line are the Breakwater, Stillwater, Clearwater (to and from Mobile), the Wanderer, the Foxhall, and formerly the City of Dallas, which was lost at sea not many months ago.

The Breakwater is the flagship of the fleet, and is commanded by Capt. Louis Rivara, a courteous Genowese mariner, and a lineal descendant of the great navigator Columbus. He is assisted by Mr. Wm. Grant, purser, who does all within his power to make the trip on his boat a pleasant and instructive one.

The Stillwater is next in importance and is commanded by Capt. Henry Galt, with Mr. L. Harang purser. The Clearwater is next, with Capt. McFarland on the bridge and Mr. J. Lowe purser. Next is the Foxhall, Capt. Leslie in charge and Mr. Wm. Macheca in charge of accounts. The Wanderer completes the list of vessels, with Capt. Brown in command and Mr. W. Wasson, purser. All of these gentlemen have sailed the ocean blue for many years, and passengers on either vessel will be given every attention, and meet with that true bon homme that stamps the true mariner.

The voyage from New Orleans is via Belize and Livingston, the steamer arriving in Baiize on Sunday night. Leaving Belize, a run of twenty-four hours down the bay brings the vessel to Livingston, where connection is made with steamboats running up Rio Dulce and across Lake Izabal to Panzos. From Livingston the vessel crosses the bay (nine miles) to Puerto Barrios, when the voyage to Guatemala ends. The vessel proceeds to Puerto Cortez, in Honduras, and begins its return trip to New Orleans. arriving on Monday evening.

On leaving the vessel at Puerto Barrios passengers proceed by mail to Gualin, a distance of 80 miles. The railroad is now complete and in operation to that point—the fare is 4 cents per mile. From Gualan the trip to Guatemala City is made by mule train and is completed in three days. The fare is $20.

From this it will be seen that instead of a sea voyage of fourteen days the traveler now reaches the capital

city in eight days, with an interesting
overland trip after the sea voyage.

RAILROADS.

It was only in recent years that
Guatemala made anything like progress in railroad building. In 1871 a
concession was granted for a railroad
This was granted to Messrs. Leland
Standferd, C. P. Huntington and others. The road was not opened to trafic
however until 1880. The line is seventy-one miles long, and connects the
capital with the Pacific Ocean. From
Champirico to Ratallhullen, a distance
of twenty-five miles, a road is operated
by the government, and arrangements
have been perfected to extend it fur-
ther north. These two lines were, up
to 1884, the only railroads in the state.

In 1884 the Guatemala Northern,
from Puerto Barrios to Guatemala
City, was begun. This was under the
direction of President Barrios, the el-
der, who with his own hands threw
the first spade of dirt that marked the
beginning. Work continued for about
twelve months, when it was brought
to an abrupt close by the declaration
of war and subsequent death of President Barrios on the battle field.

In 1888 a contract was made with
an English company to complete the
line, but it amounted to nothing.
Later, in 1889, another contract was

made with a French company, who also failed to carry out their plans.

During the operations of the English company in 1..s there was an American engineer employed on the work. At the breaking out of the war this man left the country and joined the Panama Canal Company. When the expose of that company came the American returned to Guatemala. The present President Barrios was then in charge, and at his request the American reported officialy as to the practicability of completing the line begun by the former President. As nothing was impossible to this man, he, at the request of President Barrios, took charge of the work and built eighty miles. This American was Sylvanus Miller, the man now in charge of the road.

This road is now under the general management of Mr. Miller A. Smith, a competent and popular railroad manager.

Track laying has just been completed between Gualan and Zacapa, and grading from Zacapa on toward the capital is now under way, under direction of the leading contractors, Messrs. R. H. May, Fred Prescott, Clay Parks, Wm. Penny and R. E. Caldwell.

From San Jose, on the Pacific side, a line is in operation to Guatemala City, a distance of seventy-one miles.

This is the Huntington system.

Another short line is operated by the government from Camprico to Ratalhulan.

PROPOSED LINES.

Thus far mention has been made only of the lines in operation. The system of proposed lines is extensive, and when completed will give Guatemala a most complete railroad system. As already mentioned, the line from Gualan to Guatemala City is in course of construction. In addition to this, a line is being built from Panzos to Coban, under direction of Mr. Geo. Jeckeyl, thus connecting the coffee interest of that section with navigation through Lake Izabel to Livingston. From Panzos a line will be built south to Zacapa, and from Zacapa to Jutiapa, through Jalapa. From Coban the line starts south, and is surveyed into Guatemala City and from the city to S. Geromino, on the coast.

From Zacapa another line croses to Honouras and connects with the Inter-Oceanic at S. Baraba.

When these lines are all complete the rich agricultural portions of the state will be open to commerce, and ample facilities afforded to handle the products, all of which wil be brought into Puerto Barrios for export. Guatamala can then boast of one of the most complete as well as extensive railway systems extant, and the three factors in bringing this about will be: President Barrios, for his enterprise and patriotism; Sylvanus Miller, for his ability as an engineer and contractor, and the Macheca line, for facilities in shipping and handling material.

In addition to the railroads, the country abounds in trails and roads throughout all the sections not touched by rail. All the cities and towns are connected by these public highways, and, where no rail facilities are to be had, traders and settlers will have no trouble in going from town to town.

GENERAL INFORMATION.

To the hustling investor, Gautemaula offers superior inducements, and the capital required is more in the line of "willingness" than money. The cultivation of coffee has made immense fortunes for all those who have engaged in it, and this fact has caused the inhabitants and those who cared to work, to neglect the lesser lines of work. This refers to the food supply, or articles of home consumption. All of which are neglected and will give vast returns to "small investors" who uses his brain as well as brawn.

Everything the people eat is im-

ported. Beef, vegetables, grain, fruit,
etc., are bought, not raised. Here there
is an opening for men of moderate
means. Cattle are shiped to the state
by hundreds for beef, and yet the
whole state, with its natural pas-
tures and its even climate is a natural
stock farm. Watermelons are shipped
from New Orleans, and sell for $1 each
in the various cities of the state, and
yet the soil and climate produce the
largest and best melons to be had in
any clime. Vegetables of all kinds are
shipped in, and command better prices
and find readier sale than in the
United States. Yet the best gardeners
in the world can be had in Guatemala.
The same conditions exist in dairy
products, wine, chocolate, honey, and
all those little things so common and
so necessary in the United States. The
reason for this is found in the fact
that those who are able to buy de-
vote their time and money to coffee,
and the poorer clases are too indo-
lent to raise and sell an article that
they consider useless, because not necessary to sustain life

Tobacco culture is another branch
that cannot fail to pay. This industry is specially protected by the government. and premiums are offered
for the largest amount raised by each
planter. Every native who raises five
or more "cargas" of tobacco is ex-
empt from military or municipal duty.

A 'cargas" is about one hundred pounds.

The country around Zacapa and Chiquimula is the tobacco growing portion of the state.

The articles of food that are imported because the natives will not raise them is as follows: Wheat, barley, potatoes, corn, beans, rice, hay, lard, salt and dairy products.

Guatemala is very rich in minerals. Silver and gold is found in paying quantities almost all over the state. Detailed particulars of this branch can be had by application to the government or any agent of the country. The minerals include silver, gold, salt, chalk, quicksilver, lead, copper, mica, etc. All these can be worked in paying quantities, and the mining laws of the etate are liberal and encouraging to prospectors.

Foreigners on arriving in the territory are strictly enjoined to respect the authorities and to obey the laws, for by so doing they acquire the right ot being protected by them.

Neither natives nor foreigners can claim indemnity for damages or injury to their property or person, caused by revolution.

Property is declared inviolable. Expropriation proceedings can be instituted only for motives of public interest, legally; process, in which case, the owner may receive full value of his property in current money.

Every service which, by virtue of law, cannot be rendered gratuitously, shall be properly remunerated.

No one can be arrested or imprisoned except for offense against the government. Every person arrested shall be examined within forty-eight hours. The detention shall not exceed five days; within that time the authorities shall justify the imprisonment or set the prisoner at liberty.

The government of every department, or county, is exercised by a political chief. Each town is controlled by a local authority, who is under the county officer.

In order to obtain concessions for building, privileges to cut timber or any other enterprise, application must be made to the government.

There is a generally accepted belief among those who do not post themselves, that Guatemala is a "fever breeding death trap." They think and believe that to go to that country means to expose themselves to death and sickness. This is a very mistaken idea, as nothing of the kind exists. There is no "swamp" in Guatemala; no marshes; no stagnant water or "boggs." The country being mountainous, is well drained, and the air is pure. The strip of country along the coast, varying in width from three to ten miles, is low and hot. During the months of July, August and September rain falls daily during this period. This is what is called the "rainy season." Along the coast the dampness and extreme heat during these months make it very unpleasant for foreigners, and this strip is where the fever makes its appearance. Everyone who goes there is by no means liable to sickness, the fever appearing only among those who remain in that part five or six months. Back from the coast the high land begins, and settlers are not subjected to the same conditions as along the coast.

American Consuls are stationed at the principal points.

Parties going about the country and leaving the state must have a "pass port." This can be had from any of the Consulates.

Any article of wearing apparel, food, tools, etc., can be purchased in the state. The prices are about the same as in the United States.

prepared for cold nights Parties g

Parties going to Guatemala should go prepared for cold nights, as the temperature falls, and travelers and settlers sleep under two or more blankets. If they intend to stop along the coast they should take a mosquito bar.

Blankets and bars command good prices.

Doctors. hospitals, etc., can be found without trouble in case of need.

COMMERCIAL ADVANTAGES.

In his annual report to the Secretary of State. dated January 18, 1891, Mr. Samuel Kimberly, the United States consul-general, submitted much information of value concerning the commercial opportunites for the merchants and manufacturers of the United States in Guatemala, from which a considerable portion of this chapter is compiled.

The merchants throughout the interior of the country are usually dealers in general merchandise, that is, they carry mixed stocks of goods, comprising a little of everything that is wanted by the people, nine-tenths of whom are agriculturists and laborers, and require the cheaper grades of clothing and dress goods, crockery, etc. Their capital is usually small and they procure their supplies from the wholesale dealers in the larger cities of the Republic, carrying stocks representing a value of from $5,000 to $15,000, about one-half of which is purchased on credit from six to nine months' time, with interest of 7, 9, and 10 per cent. The goods are transported from Guatemala city and other commercial centers on pack mules, ox carts, and by "cargadores"—men who carry packs on their back—and take loads of 125 pounds. A mule carries 250 pounds, but the load must be divided into two packages of 125 pounds each to be handled conveniently. For this reason manufacturers and exporters in the United States should observe the greater care in the packing of articles for that market, making the packages not heavier in weight than 125 pounds, as secure and compact as possible and without any unnecessary weight. The same conditions apply to Mexico, and all the countries of Central and South America.

There is general complaint throughout all the American Republics about the carelessness of packing in the United States, and for that reason much trade goes to Europe where packing has been reduced to a fine art. It is particularly necessary that goods for Guatemala and other Central American countries should be carefully packed because of the rough hadling they receive on the Isthmus of Panama, and at San Jose, and Champerico, the two Pacific seaports of Guatemala.

Merchants in the larger cities of Guatemala carry stocks valued from $25,000 to $100,000.

In his report, Consul-General Kimberly says: "That there need be no

apprehension as to collections, for 1
have discovered that business failures
are exceedingly rare, and fraudulent
business failures are unknown here.
In fact, the laws of this Republic are
of such a stringent character that one
having failed in business must show
to the legal authority that he has fully
paid off all previous liability before
he can recommence. The merchants,
and especially the larger houses, are
as a rule thoroughly strict and reliable, and are composed of all nation-
alities, the Germans, however, predom-
inating."

WEIGHTS AND MEASURES.

The standard of weight adopted is
the Spanish pound. One libra is six-
teen ounces; one aroba is twenty-five
pounds.

In measuring distance the Spanish
vera is the standard. A "vera" is three
feet. Five thousand veras is equal to
4,180 kilomenters, and constitute a
league, or three English miles.

MONEY.

The national standard for money is
the dollar, which contains 900 grains
of silver.

A peso, or dollar, is worth 100 cents.
A pesata is 25 cents; a real is worth
$12\frac{1}{2}$ cents; a medio is $6\frac{1}{4}$ cents; a
cuartillo is $3\frac{1}{8}$ cents. There is also in
circulation 15 and 10 cent pieces.

MAILS.

Guatemala entered the Universal Postal Union in 1881. The mail service is perfectly organized, according to the best systems in operation. Residents and visitors will have no trouble in receiving and forwarding mail matter. The rates are as follows: Letters, 5 cents; papers, 1 cent.

TELEGRAPH.

The state has a fine telegraph system. Lines bringing all the principal points of the state into communication. There is estimated to be about 3,000 miles of telegraph lines in operation. The rates are about the same as in the United States. All messages are sent in Spanish.

MINES AND MINING.

Guatemala is very rich in mines and minerals. Gold and silver is mined in paying quantities, but the method is crude and primitive, most of it being "placier." The mines are scattered all over the state and along the Guatemala Northern Railway there are very rich deposits and operated mines. It is liberal in its mining laws and in fact offers inducements for their development.

The following provisions of the law will give a correct idea of the manner of acquiring and working mines.

Auriferous sands, iron deposits,
etc., in river beds or placiers, on
whatever land they may be found are
free to all persons without special per-
mit.

All persons, either native or foreign
who shall discover a deposit, ledge
or vein shall be entitled to the concession thereof.

All persons who shall work old or
abandoned mines shall be considered
as discoverer, and shall be entitled to
the undisputed possession.

These are the main features govern-
ing prospectors. Claims for "blind
leads," etc., are about the same as in
the United States. A copy of themin-
ing laws can be had by application to
the government.

EDUCATION.

For some years past the government
of Guatemala has cultivated with the
greatest care the development of public instruction, which is free of charge
and compulsory. There are 1252
schools throughout the Republic.

In addition to these, the Republic
has "A National Library," containing
30,000 volumes.

A Conservatory of Music and fourteen schools of music; all maintained
at a cost of about $7,000.

There are three schools of Arts and
Trades, employing ten professors and
thirty foremen in the wor. sho .

Recently the government has author-
ized the establishment of one of these
schools for women.

The government has established six
Central Technical Colleges, viz: The
Law School; The College of Medicine
and Pharmacy and the College of Engineers—two of each.

LABOR.

The shipping of negro laborers from New Orleans to Guatemala has been a matter of serious importance during the last few years.

The Guatemala Northern Railroad system has been virtually worked by said labor, which labor, four years ago, when Sylvanus Miller was constructing the road himself; the negroes then flocked from every Southern State crowding the labor agencies for shipment to Guatemala, for work on said road. Unfortunately, among them were some lazy, worthless, barrel-house negroes, who, being under the constant surveillance of the police, and liable to arrest here, preferred to be shipped to Guatemala. Said negroes, intending to pursue the same course of life over there refused to work; hence trouble ensued between them and the contractors.

Those negroes, gamblers by trade, out of their first earnings, bought their tickets and returned here. Awful have been their tales of ill-treatment and starvation by the management of the contractors. Their imaginary wrongs, with their false statements published in the press, to the gross injustice of their employers.

These lying statements have caused a bugbear among the better class of negroes, who under no circumstances could be induced to go. Others, still, on the contrary, have come back to see their friends here, and have willingly returned there.

In speaking about starvation, the following weekly list of provisions furnished by Mr. S. Miller to laborers at the cost of 50 cents per day, in Guatemala money,, which is equal to 25 cents United States currency, will prove the falsity of said statements:

2 pounds fresh meat.
3 pounds smoked sides
2 pounds salt beef.
5 pounds flour.
5pounds cornmeal.
2 pounds beans.
2 pounds rice.
1pound lard.
2 pounds brown sugar .
1 pound onions.
1 pound dried apples.
1-4 pound tea.
1-4 pound coffee.

The same trouble exists with some "hobos" who go on transportation with the sole purpose of visiting the country at he expense of the contractors, and as they are compelled to work out their transportation, they complain like the negroes.

The contractors want he men; they pay the wages, hence they want the work for it.

The wages paid to laborers and mechanics are as follows:

Laborers for railroad work—$3.00 per day.

Section foremen—$150 per month.

Conductors —$150 per month, with board.

Brakemen—$109 per month, with board.

Engineers—From $7.00 to $9.90 per day, no board.

Firemen—$3.00 per day, no board.

Machinists—From $6.00 to $8.00 per day, no board.

House and bridge carpenters—From $5.00 to 7.00 per day, according to their ability.

Sawmill laborers—$2.00 to $3.00 per day, no board.

Sawmill mechanics—$5.00 to $6.60 per day, no board.

Timbermen and ox-drivers—From 3.00 to $5.00, no board.

Hewers—From $15.00 to $16.06 per 1000 board measure, no board.

Ties—6x8, 7 feet long, left at the stump, 40 cents each, no board.

Laborers for rock work—$3.00 per day, no board.

Stonecutters—$6.00 to $8.00 per day, no board.

All wages are paid in Guatemala money.

Board can be had at the following rates: 50 cents, 75 cents, $1.00 and $1.50 per day, also in Guatemala money.

Rock work by contract—$1.25 per cubic yard, and 15 cents extra for filling.

ADVICE TO LABORERS.

Laborers and mechanics, when shipped on transportation, must not misrepresent their occupation when they apply for shipment to Guatemala; otherwise they will be the sufferers.

There is plenty of railroad, rock and timber work for all classes of laborers and mechanics.

Work is not compulsory in Guatemala, unless the transportation ticket is paid; when then the laborer is at liberty to work wherever and for whoever he pleases. Therefore be careful to abide in good faith by the above advice; otherwise you will be subject to arrest.

If possible, pay your own transportation, as you will then be under no obligation to either employer or contractor, and you will feel the benefit of it.

EXHIBITION.

By act of the Legislators of Guatemala, Central America, of May the 8th, 1894. it was decided for President Barrios to open the first exhibition at Guatemala City on the 15th day of March, 1897, and close the same on the 15th. day of July following.

The exhibition will be held in the Exhibition Building, covering twelve block, 8082 square miles.

The exhibition will comprise all branches of Science, Art, Industry and the natural products of the five Republics of Central America.

All articles sent to this exhibition should bemarked Exhibition Bunlding, Central America, and should be well packed, for the committee will only be responsible for articles received in good condition. All articles sent to this exhibition will be free from duty.

No rent or space will be charged for any article sent to this exhibition.

Reduced rates will be given by all railroad and steamship companies for all articles sent to this exhibition.

Fifteen thousand dollars in cash prizes will be given away to winners of different articles. Also, gold, silver and bronze medals.

In making application for space for exhibit, the number, size and nature of the objects must be stated. All aplications must be made to the Central Committee, which committee will clear through any of the customhouse of the Republic of Guatemala all articles addressed to the Central American Exhibition.

Prices to the exhibition is 25 cents,
children under 10 years of age free.
Many are the advantages to be gained
by seeing this exhiibtion. It will bring
many objects together, so we may compare them; we shall learn what we do
not know, and improve what we already
know. We may communicate to others
a knowledge of their production, and it
will thus awaken human labor.

DISTANCES.

For the benefit of anyone who intend
to emigrate to Guatemala, the following
information taken from the Geua del
Immigrante, published in Guatemala,
in June, 1896, is here given:

The distances btween the capital of the
Republic and the heads of departments
are to the: To the Antigua (department
of Sacatepeguy), 9 leagues or 27 miles; to
Chimaltenaugo (department of same
name), 12 leagues or 36 miles; to Amatit-
ian, (department of same name), 6
leagues or 18 miles; to Escuintla, 14 1-2
leagues or 43 1-2 miles; to Cuaziniguilapa
(Santa Rosa), 14 leagues or 42 miles; to
Solola, 30 leagues or 90 miles.

To Totonicapau, 37 leagues or 111 miles;
to Quezaltnaugo, 40 leagues or 120 miles;
to Mazatenaugo (Sechitepeguez), 46
leagues or 120 miles; to Retalhuleu, 51
leagues or 153 miles; to San Marco, 55
leagues or 165 miles; to Huchuetenaugo,
65 leagues or 195 miles; to Santa Cruz del
Quiche, 32 leagues or 96 miles; to Salama
(Bajaverapez), 23 leagues or 69 miles; to
Coban (Alta Verapaz), 42 leagues or 126

miles; to Flores (Peten), 107 leagues or
321 miles; to Izabal, 72 leagues or 216
miles; to Zacapa, 42 leagues or 126 miles;
to Chiquimula, 45 leagues or 136 miles;
to Jalapa. 25 lcagnes or 87 miles..

EXPORTATION.

Coffee is the pricipal article of exportation and to prove the increase of this
indwustry it is only necessary to notice
the following tables, taken from the official documents from 1883 to 1893, a period
of ten years:

	Value.
1883..	$4,848,832 68
1893..	18,550,518 73

As will be seen by the above state-
ment there has been an increase in the
exportation of coffee in a period of ten
years of $13,700,686 05—a magnificent
showing. All of the work was done by
native labor. How much more would
have been achieved by American skilled
laborers.

LEMON CULTURE.

Lemon culture in Guatemala has been entirely neglected by the inhabitants of that country, although no part of America has been so favored by nature for the successful cultivation of this fruit. A lemon grove could be brought in to bearing in less than half the time it requires in any other portion of this continent by a method we shall proceed to explain. The lime tree grows wild all over Central America, and especially in Guatemala. They grow in all parts of the Republic, from the sea level to an altitude of 5000 feet above it. The fruit is small (about the size of an English walnut) but very juicy. By grafting the Sicilian, California or Florida lemon in-c these trees, a bearing grove in five and a half or six years, may be looked for The trees need very little cultivation and in seting out a grove it is only necessary to plant fifteen feet apart, and keep the ground clean around the roots Grafting is done by splits or by-shields The latter is more generally in use, and the proper season is in the month of May or October. The first method is called "sleeping eye," because it is necessary to wait till the spring to see whether the grafting has been successful. The latter is practiced by the most intelligent growers and is called the "living eye" for the reason that should it fail in the coming fall it is operated on again.

The shoots are to be chosen from the best and most vigorous lemon trees, and in the fifth or sixth year, one may have

a fine bearing lemon grove, fruiting all
the year round. A ten-year-old tree pro-
duces 500 lemons, while at fifteen 1000 is
an ordinary yield. Pruning is done ac
cording to the growth of the tree. The
method most generally in use is an in-
verted cone. This form is obtained by
cutting down the main trunk, and let-
ting the lateral branches grow in order
to have all the ventilation and sunlight
possible.

This would be the best paying industry, next to coffee, without any doubt,
when we consider that over one million
boxes of lemons are imported annually
from Sicily alone to this State The
numbers we receive from Spain and the
South of France are not included in the
calculation.

This profitable industry awaits only the
skilful hand of the American emigrant
to give it the impetus it deserves. The
same remark applies to oranges, which,
in Guatemala and Honduras, grow the
year round, and are exported to this
country in crates one-half of them rot-
ting for want of careful packing.

HONDURAS.

While Guatemala is making tremen-
dous strides in railroad building and
general grogress, Honduras, her sister
republic, has not been idle. A concession has been granted to a northern
syndicate for the building of two railroad systems; the Inter-Oceanic and
the Puerto Cortez Truxillo line, which
will, like the Northern of Guatemala,
connect the two shores of the state,
and open to settlers and investors the
vast agricultural and mineral wealth
of the state.

In the line of possibilities thus
opened, Honduras will outrank Guatemala in importance of the fruit products, being peculiarly adapted to
the cultivation of all tropical fruits.

Foremost among the fruits of Honduras is the banana, which grows
wild all over the valleys of the state.
In years gone by thousands of tons of
these bananas ripened and rotted on
the tree, because there was no one to
cut them, and no merchant to buy.
Now all is changed.

Two firms, to whom full credit must

be given, opened the fruit trade between
Honduras and America, and to whom
Honduras is indebted for having led
other enterprising Americans to go to
Honduras and take advantage of nature's rich gifts. Now the delicious
fruit of the Honduras fields are
brought almost daily to our doors.

The banana, now so plentiful and
well known, is comparatively new in
the fruit market, dating back only
about thirty years. At the beginning
transportation facilities were so limited that it was impossible to bring the
fruit to market in anything like sale-
able condition; the transportation was
confined to small sailing vessels, and
the length of time required to make
the voyage permitted the fruit to
ripen and spoil before the vessel
reached port. The supply was, therefore, limited, and was barely enough
to supply the small city trade of New
Orleans, and the sale was mostly to
negroes and the lower classes.

About 1866 a steamer was put in the
trade. This vessel was chartered by a
company known as the "Black Ball"
line. After two years of unsuccessful
business the company dissolved. Sal-
vado and Joseph Otari, stockholders
in the company, then bought a steamer and began the business in their
own names. This was the first line
to Central America, and is now known
as the "Pioneer Line."

Soon after the Otari line started **the Macheca Brothers** began **the same** business, and **these two firms** virtually forced the people of **the Northern cities to** recognize **the banana as a staple** article. They appointed agents in all the principal cities and pushed the business to its present immense proportions.

Following the Macheca line came:

The Bocas del Toro and Colon line.

The Costa Rica line.

The Campania Agricola Mechantile.

The Carribbean Banana Company.

An amusing incident, illustrating how **little** was known of the banana at **that time** is shown by the following **experience of** Mr. V. Lamantia, of **New Orleans:**

In 1864 he shipped fifty bunches of **bananas** from New Orleans to St. **Louis; the fruit cost** him at New Orleans $5.00 per bunch. At St. Louis he was unable **to** find buyers, and re-**shipped to** Louisville, Ky. Here he **again failed to** get dealers **to handle the fruit, and** in order **to reach the people** he opened **a stand in the market** and tried **to sell at retail. As no one** knew what a banana was, **a** crowd would gather and such questions as "What are those things?" "Where did you get them?" "How do you eat them?" etc., was asked. In order **to** answer them he hired a boy to **cry** the fruit and **to eat some of it be-**

fore the **crowd.** Occasionaly one would be induced to **taste** it in a hesitating manner, **and the** verdict was usually an uncertain shake of the head. '**As a result of this uphill** business the fruit ripened and spoiled, and was thrown away. This was the state of the banana trade in 1864. Compare this with the present enormous business, and a correct idea of the growth of the banana business can be had.

The steamship lins now bring to New Orleans millions of bunches, to say nothing of the trade through New York, Boston, Philadelphia and Mobile, all of which dates its beginning from the Oteri Brothers' first venture.

In Central America there are thousands of acres of land suitable for banana culture, and waiting for settlers who is now always sure of a market for his crop.

Honduras has now one line of railway in operation, running from Puerto Cortez to San Pedro. This line does a good fruit business, and will be taken up by the Inter-Oceanic.

DUTIES ON IMPORTS.

The tariff of Guatemala as here printed is the latest official publication of that country; but a number of decrees modifying the same have been issued, principal among which is the one promulgated October 23, 1885, augmenting the duties 20 per cent on all merchandise imported into the country; consequently that percentage should be added to these rates.

The Guatemalan peso was valued by the Director of the Mint of the United States October 1, 1891, at 72.3 cents.

SECTION I.

Articles Prohibited.

Bullets, iron or lead, bombs, hand grenades and other projectiles of war.

Cannons or other pieces of artillery.

Carbines, rifles or muskets, military.

Counterfeit money.

Machinery and materials for coining or printing money.

Nitrate of potash, or saltpetre, exceeding 25 pounds.

Nitro-glycerine and dynamite.

Obscene pictures, books or objects, and such as are contrary to good morals and customs.

Powder of all kinds, exceeding 2 pounds.

Tobacco leaf.

Tobacco, manufactured, exceeding 5 pounds.

Merchandise imported into the Republic is divided into six classes:

(1) Free list.

(2) Articles paying 10 per cent.

(3) Articles paying 25 per cent.

(4) Articles paying 70 per cent.

(5) Trade with the Central American

Republics.

(6) Trade with the Mexican Republic.

The appraisements established in this code shall be the basis for the collection of import duties.

SECTION II.
Free List.

Anchors and hauling lines.

Animals, live, for breeding, or stuffed.

Articles imported by the government or municipalities for public use or for charitable institutions

Articles imported for their own use by diplomatic ministers residing in the Republic, providing the privilege is reciprocal and the provisions of this code are complied with Consuls and vice-consuls do not enjoy the exemption

Baggage of passengers, the term including all articles of personal use and indispensable instruments belonging to the profession or business of the owner in proportion to his station and circumstances; also furniture in use by parties intending to establish themselves in the country.

Beans.

Boats, tackle, sails, chains, and other equipments for vessels, for use in the ports and on the lakes of the Republic.

Books, used.

Bricks, fire, and crucibles for smelting.

Buildings, frame or iron, complete.

Cement, Roman, or hydraulic lime.

Coal.

Corn.

Crucibles and other apparatus for assaying metals.

Diamonds and other precious tones, unset.

Fragments and rigging of shipwrecked vessels.

Fuse, for mines.

Gas, apparatus for making.

Gold and silver in bars, dust, or coined.

Guano and other fertilizers.

Hay and other feed not specified.

Iron, pig, or in bulk, in quantities not less than 5 pounds.

Lodestone.

Lumber, rough.

Machinery, unknown in the country, and applicable to industry or agriculture.

Minerals, refuse.

Models of machines and buildings.

Molds for making flowers.

Pease, dried.

Periodicals, loose or bound.

Photographs and views of the country.

Plants, exotic, and their seeds.

Portraits belonging to families residing in the country.

Potatoes.

Quicksilver.

Rice.

Rye.

Samples of goods the duty on which shall not exceed $1.

Seeds, flower, vegetable, or other kind not specified in this chapter.

Telegraphic supplies.

Vegetables, fresh.

Wharves in the ports, appliances for.

Wire, barbed, for fences, with hooks.

Wrappings, ordinary, when the articles are not appraised on the gross weight:
In bales, the wrapping cloth, oiled

cloth, side boards **and** straps **are** considered as wrappings. In cases, **the** tin or zinc lining, cardboard, paper and casings, unless expressly included in the corresponding appraisement. No blanket, sheet or other article mentioned in sections 4 and 5 of this chapter will be considered as wrapping.

The following articles are also free of duty, as per proclamation of the President of the United States of America, dated October (1) 1890:

1. Live animals.
2. Barley, corn or maize, and rye.
3. Cornmeal.
4. Potatoes. peas and beans.
5. Fresh vegetables.
6. Rice.
7. Hay and straw for forage.
8. Tar, pitch, resin, turpentine and asphalt. ●
9. Cotton-seed oil and other products of said seed.
10. Quicksilver.
11. Mineral coal.
12. Guano and other fertilizers.
13. Lumber and timber, in the rough or prepared for building purposes.
14. Houses of wood or iron, complete or in parts.
15. Fire-brick, lime, cement, shingles and tiles of clay or glass for roofing, and construction of buildings.
16. Marble in slabs, columns, cornices, door and window frames and fountains, and dressed or undressed marble for buildings.
17. Piping of clay, glazed or unglazed, for acqueducts and sewers.

8. Wire, plain or barbed, for fences, with hooks and staples for same.

19. Printed books, bound or unbound; printed music; maps, charts and globes.

20. Materials for the construction and equipment of railways.

21. Materials for electrical illumination.

22. Materials expressly for the construction of wharves.

23. Anchors and hoisting tackle.

24. Railings of cast or wrought iron.

25. Balconies of cast or wrought iron.

26. Window blinds of wood or metal.

2. Iron fire-places or stoves.

28. Machinery, including steam machinery for agriculture and mining, and separate parts for the same.

29. Gold and silver, in bullion, dust or coin.

SECTION III.
Articles Paying 10 Per Cent on Invoice Valuation.

Acids, used in the arts and industries of the country, not included in the tariff on drugs and medicses.

Artificial teeth.

Axles, tires and wheels for wagons, carts or wheelbarrows.

Barley.

Barometers.

Barrels, pipes and hogsheads, empty.

Bellows, blacksmiths'.

Books, for exercise in writing, drawing and mathematics, for use of schools.

Candle molds.

Cane, rattan, straw and palm leaf, for furniture or hats.

Caldrons or boilers, iron or copper, for

sugar mills.

Charts or maps, geographical

Checks, metal, for use on haciendas.

Clocks for towers, with dials and bells.

Compasses, mariners'.

Cotton, raw, with or without seed.

Crucibles.

Felt roofing or any invention for roofs.

Fur, rabiit ro hare, for hat-making.

Globes, geographical or astronomical, for study, all kinds.

Hoops, wood or ron, for barrels, hogsheads, etc.

Horsehair.

Hour-glasses.

Instruments used in the sciences, arts, and agriculture, not otherwise classified in this code.

Jewelry, gold at least .600 fine, silver at least .835 fine.

Lasts, for boots and shoes; blocks, for wigs and hats, wood.

Lead in bulk or in sheets for roofs.

Levels

Lightning rods and appliances.

Linear measures.

Lithographic stone.

Lumber, for building.

Machinery for agriculture, mining and other arts, sciences and industries, and loose pieces belonging to same.

Marble, rough, in bulk.

Mausoleums or sarcophagi.

Mathematical instrument cases.

Music, printed and manuscript.

Needles, knitting.

Oil or haircloth for making hats.

Paper, stamped for embroidery.

Paper, for printing, in sheets at least 100

x65 centimeters.

Patterns for tailors and dressmakers.

Pipes, iron, lead or zinc, for conducting water, gas, etc.

Platform scales for weighing over 5,000 pounds.

Plows of all kinds.

Poison, for curing hides.

Presses, hydraulic, for extracting oil or for use in the agricultural industry.

Printed books.

Printers' ink.

Printing office materials.

Pulleys or blocks, wood or iron.

Pumps, iron, with or without piping, for mines, irrigation or fires.

Sheet iron for roofs.

Slate for oofs.

Statues, life-size, for models.

Staves, barrel.

Sugar molds.

Surgical instrument cases.

Table service, silver at least .835 fine gold at least .600 fine.

Tar of all kinds.

Type for printing.

Wagons or carts of all kinds, and their appliances, except harness.

Watches, gold at least .600 fine, silver at least .835 fine.

Wheat.

Wheelbarrows of all kinds.

Wire masks for emptying bee-hives.

Wool, carded and uncarded.

Zinc in bars.

SECTION IV.

Articles Paying 25 Per Cent on Appraised Valuation.

Dollars

and other dressed hides, except patent leather, not mentioned in this code, including paper wrappings, pound.... 289

Pianos—

  Grand, each.. .. ..506.10

  Half grand, each.. ....289.20

  Upright, all kinds, each.. .. ....216.90

  Square, triple-stringed, each....202.44

  Square, double-stringed, each... 72.30

  Square, single-stringed, or mon-
    ochord, each.... .. .. 21.69

  Sacks, empty, for exporting pro-
    ducts of the country, each....   .145

  Steel, in bars or sheets, un-
    wrought, gross weight, 100
    pounds.... ....   4.338

Thread—

  Cotton, or yarn and wicking, un-
    bleached or bleached, for weav-
    ing, gross weight, pound.... ..   .145

  Same, red cotton, gross weight,
    pound.. 362

  Same, other colors, gross weight,
    pound.... 264

Tin, in bars, or sheets, gross
  weight, 100 pounds......., ...   7.23

Tin plate, gross weight, pound....   .043

Worsted, for embroidery or knitting, including weight of wrapping, pound.... 723

Each and every article not enumerated in the above articles I, II, III, IV, pay 70 of 100 ad valorem.

Articles whose appraisement raises a doubt by reason of their size, make, quality, or classification shall be appraised the same as articles of a similar character.

Articles not specified in this title which are not similar to any enumerated will pay 70 per cent on their invoice valuation.

THE AGENCY.

In speaking of Guatemala and her future, nothing has as yet been said about the prime factor in her development. This is the labor, or immigration agency. This agency is located at No. 327 Exchange Alley, and is the only one in New Orleans; is under $5,000 bond as required by law.

The agency supplies contractors with labor of all kinds, and give true and reliable information to travelers and those wanting to know about the country represented.

All letters of inquiry will receive prompt attention and all information given can be relied upon implicitly.

☞ Copies of this Book, together with Maps, etc., and any information desired, can be had by addressing

V. LAMANTIA,

327 Exchange Alley,

NEW ORLEANS, LA.

CENTRAL AMERICA

Railroad and Ticket Agency

FAIR WARNING.

This **Agency** ships **Laborers** and Mechanics to Guatemala, for Railroad and Timber work, when so ordered by Contractors who then advance their transportation, and same is deducted from the first wages.

When we call for **Stationmen,** (**Diggers,**) **Rockmen, Masons, Stone Cutters, House** or **Bridge Carpenters, Wood Choppers, Trackmen, Tiemakers** or **Machinists, etc.,** we mean men who understand their business, able to do the work and make money by it. And no **Cooks, Waiters, Clerks, Book** or **Timekeepers, Bakers,** Cake or Pastrymen, **Tailors, Barbers** or Shoemakers need apply for same.

Parties misrepresenting their trade when they apply for shipment to this Agency, will be put to work at anything, until their transportation is paid for. when they will be at liberty to work at whatever they please. Hence, we want the right sort of men we call for, and no others.

V. LAMANTIA.

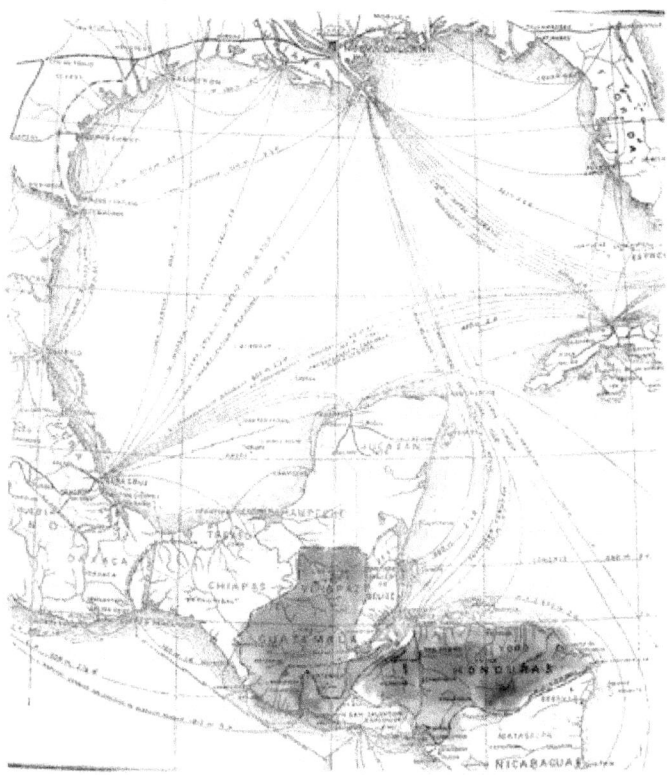

LATEST RAILROADS
MAP OF GUATEMALA AND HONDURAS.

GUATEMALA

(text illegible)

STEAMSHIP SCHEDULE.

(text illegible)

MEXICO

BRITISH HONDURAS

CARIBBEAN SEA

GULF OF HONDURAS

HONDURAS

SALVADOR

NICARAGUA

PACIFIC OCEAN

EXPLANATION

ISSUED BY THE
CENTRAL AMERICA RAILROAD AGENCY,

A. LAMANTIA, Agent.   327 Exchange Alley.   New Orleans, La.

www.ingramcontent.com/pod-product-compliance
Lightning Source LLC
Chambersburg PA
CBHW031747090426
42739CB00008B/911